THE CHANGING FACE OF
RUSSIA

Text by GALYA RANSOME
Photographs by BOB SMITH

Raintree

Chicago, Illinois

© Copyright 2004 Raintree

Published by Raintree, a division of Reed Elsevier, Inc.
Chicago, Illinois
Customer Service 888-363-4266
Visit our website at www.raintreelibrary.com

Copyright Permissions
Raintree
100 N. Lasalle
Suite 1200
Chicago, IL 60602

Library of Congress Cataloging-in-Publication Data:
Ransome, Galya.
  Russia / Galya Ransome.
     v. cm. -- (The changing face of--)
Includes bibliographical references and index.
Contents: St. Petersburg : northern capital -- Past times -- Landscape and climate -- Natural resources -- The changing environment -- The changing population -- Changes at home -- Changes at work -- The way ahead.
  ISBN 0-7398-6042-9
  1. Russia (Federation)--Juvenile literature. [1. Russia (Federation)]
I. Title. II. Series.
  DK510.23.R36 2003
  947.086--dc21
                              2003000441

Printed in Hong Kong

1 2 3 4 5 6 7 8 9 0
LB 07 06 05 04 03

The website addresses (URLs) included in this book were valid at the time of going to press. However, because of the nature of the Internet, it is possible that some addresses may have changed, or sites may have changed or closed down since publication. While the author and Publisher regret any inconvenience this may cause readers, no responsibility for any such changes can be accepted by the author, the packager, or the Publisher.

Acknowledgments
The publishers would like to thank the following for their contributions to this book: Rob Bowden—statistics research; Peter Bull—map illustration; Nick Hawken—statistics panel illustrations. All photographs are by Bob Smith except: pp. 6, 20, 44 Popperfoto; pp. 9, 10, 14, 24, 27, 34, 40, 41 Hodder Wayland Picture Library; p. 10 Eye Ubiquitous; p. 14 Corbis; p. 21 Impact Photos.

Contents

St. Petersburg: Northern Capital

The city of St. Petersburg was founded by the Russian Tsar Peter the Great in 1703 and was the capital of the Russian Empire until 1918. It is the second-largest Russian city, the largest seaport in Russia, and home to nearly five million people. St Petersburg is still known as the "northern capital."

St. Petersburg's history

During its history, St. Petersburg has seen many of the dramatic changes that have happened to Russia. In 1917 the Bolshevik Revolution began here. The revolution put the Communist party into power. The Bolsheviks murdered the tsar and his family, before taking over the country in the name of its citizens and forming the Soviet Union. In 1924 the city was renamed Leningrad, after Lenin, the leader of the revolution. During World War II, the people of Leningrad were surrounded by the Nazi army and survived a devastating two-year siege—an event that helped to defeat Adolph Hitler. After the Soviet Union collapsed in 1991, St. Petersburg's citizens voted for the city to be known again by its old name.

Changes in St. Petersburg

In the 1990s, St. Petersburg became run down because of a lack of money. Now that the economic situation has improved, buildings are being renovated or converted into shops and offices. Business and industry are beginning to grow. The city has gone through some difficult times, but it is adapting to life after Communism. Both Russia and St. Petersburg are looking forward to the future.

▲ The 18th-century Catherine Palace in Tsarskoye Selo, near St. Petersburg, one of the many palaces built for the Russian royal family.

◀ Traffic on Nevsky Prospekt, the main street of St. Petersburg. Traffic is a growing problem for many Russian cities.

▲ This map shows the main geographical features of Russia, as well as places mentioned in this book.

RUSSIA: KEY FACTS

Area: 6,592,822 square miles (17,075,400 sqare kilometers)

Population: 145 million

Population density: 22 people per square mile (8.5 people per square kilometer)

Capital city: Moscow (8.4 million)

Other main cities (municipalities): St. Petersburg (4.7 million); Novosibirsk (1.4 million); Yekaterinburg (1.3 million); Samara (1.2 million)

Highest mountain: Mount Elbrus, Caucasus (18, 510 feet, 5,642 meters)

Longest river: Lena (2,684 miles, 4,320 kilometers)

Main language: Russian

Major religions: Christianity (Russian Orthodox); Islam.

Currency: ruble (1 ruble = 100 kopeks)

Past Times

In 1917 the Russian Empire, which spanned two continents and covered about 17 percent of the world's land surface, became the world's first Communist state. Known as the Union of Soviet Socialist Republics, the Soviet Union, or the USSR, it was made up of fifteen regions called republics.

Under Communist rule

Between 1917 and 1991, the Soviet government controlled everything. All agricultural land was organized into large collective farms, where everyone worked for the state and all produce was sold by the state. Huge factories were built to supply goods for the entire Soviet Union. Needs such as employment, food, housing, and education were available to everyone, but the needs of individuals received little attention. Political and civil rights were very limited.

In 1985 Mikhail Gorbachev became Soviet leader. He launched the policies of *perestroika* (restructuring the economic and political systems) and *glasnost* (openness). Gorbachev's reforms quickly led to the collapse of the Soviet Union and the end of the Communist party's rule.

▲ Here, in Lenin's mausoleum on Red Square in Moscow, the mummified body of Lenin is still visited by thousands of people every year.

◄ U.S. president Reagan and the Soviet leader Gorbachev during one of their meetings. Gorbachev was the Soviet president most liked by Western leaders. He started perestroika and glasnost and was the last leader of the Soviet Union.

The end of Communism

In 1991 Communism ended in Russia and the other Soviet republics became independent. Boris Yeltsin was Russia's first democratically elected president; he had to reorganize the country. As the Communist system collapsed, inflation soared and crime increased. In 1999 Vladimir Putin became the president. His aims were to tackle corruption and crime and to reestablish Russia as a major world power.

▶ *Commercial advertising on billboards like this one was not allowed in the Soviet Union. Today there is as much advertising in Russia as there is in the West.*

IN THEIR OWN WORDS

My name is Svetlana Andreyevna Serova, and I am a schoolteacher. My parents lived before *perestroika*, when life was very different and easier in some ways than today. Many things have changed since 1991. Although there are more opportunities for young people, life is more difficult for older people. People can travel abroad and see foreign countries, but the majority of people can't afford it. We have to pay for medical care; for some people, this is very difficult. Our culture is changing, too. In the past, there was censorship and films seemed to be better. Now they show bad programs on TV and there are too many advertisements. I think we need more Russian traditions and more Russian music.

Landscape and Climate

Even after the collapse of the Soviet Union, Russia is still the largest country in the world, covering more than one-ninth of the world's land surface. It is nearly twice as large as the United States, and spans eleven time zones. It shares borders with many countries, including Ukraine, Finland, Kazakhstan, Mongolia, and China.

Coasts, rivers, and lakes

Russia has the longest coastline of any country— it stretches 23,280 mi (37,350 km), mainly along the Arctic and Pacific Oceans. Most of the major rivers flow into the Arctic Ocean and are frozen for up to eight months a year. The Lena River is the longest river in Russia, at 2,684 mi (4,320 km). The Ob and Irtysh Rivers form one of the largest river systems in the world.

The Volga (2,193 mi [3,530 km]), which flows into the Caspian Sea, is the longest river in Europe. It has great importance for Russia because of the many giant dams and hydroelectric power stations that have been built across it. The Caspian Sea is the world's largest saltwater lake. It covers

▲ Lake Ladoga, the largest lake in Europe, is part of a canal system that links the Baltic and White Seas.

◄ The Moscow River flows through the Russian capital, past the Kremlin, on its way toward the Volga, the longest river in Europe.

IN THEIR OWN WORDS

My name is Ulyana Lavrentyeva. I live in Akademgorodok in Siberia, outside the city of Novosibirsk. Winters in Siberia are cold but in summer it is hot. Summers could be nice if it weren't for mosquitoes. They can be really vicious! We live on the border between the taiga and the steppe. We can either go to pick mushrooms in the forest or visit lakes in the steppe. We also have a big artificial lake near our city, created when a dam was built across the Ob River. It is beautiful there, but the shoreline is slowly being eaten away by the water, which is very sad.

an area bigger than Japan. The area beneath the Caspian Sea is rich in oil, but its ownership is disputed between Russia and the other countries on its shores.

Lake Baikal in Siberia is the deepest freshwater lake in the world. It is home to thousands of animal species, including the rare freshwater seal. Because of its unique traits, Lake Baikal is a United Nations' World Heritage Site.

▼ Russia has thousands of beautiful lakes that are well stocked with fish.

Mountains and plains

The Ural Mountains divide the huge, flat plain that stretches across Russia. The Caucasus Mountains are located in the southwest, between the Black Sea and the Caspian Sea. The highest peak in the Caucasus Mountains is an extinct volcano called Mount Elbrus (18,510 feet [5,642 meters]), which is also the highest point in Europe.

◄ *The Ural Mountains are usually considered the dividing line between Europe and Asia. They stretch from the Arctic Ocean to the Caspian Sea.*

Forests and tundra

Nearly 25 percent of the world's woodlands are in Russia. Forest covers much of the northern part of Russia and Siberia, where it is known as taiga. In the far north of Siberia is tundra—a bitterly cold, treeless area where very few people live. The soil beneath the surface is called permafrost, because it is permanently frozen. The tundra has many natural resources, including oil and natural gas.

▼ *The Siberian taiga is a coniferous-forest region that lies south of the treeless Arctic tundra. It occupies 40 percent of European Russia and covers much of Siberia.*

Climate

Russia has a harsh climate that suffers from extremes of temperature. In general, winters are long and cold, and summers are short and hot—although it is colder in the north and warmer in the south. The north of Siberia is the coldest inhabited place in the world—temperatures can reach as low as -94°F (-70°C)—whereas in the south, temperatures can reach 104°F (40°C). In central Russia, winters are very cold, but summers are pleasantly warm. In recent years, there have been climate changes, which may be because of global warming. For example, it is now quite common for snow to fall and melt several times during the winter, but in the past it would have remained frozen all winter.

▲ *It rains more in the west of Russia than the east, but heavy rainfall is a fact of life in all the major cities of European Russia.*

IN THEIR OWN WORDS

My name is Ekaterina Nilovna Gromova. I am a retired engineer. I worked for many years in Murmansk in the Kola peninsula. Murmansk is the largest city and port inside the Arctic Circle. The sea never freezes there. The Murmansk region lies in two geographical zones—tundra and taiga. There are no trees in the tundra, so there is nothing to break the high winds. Winters are very cold there. Summer lasts for only 60 days and we have even had snow in August.

Natural Resources

Russia has more natural resources than any other country in the world. The major oil deposits are in western and eastern Siberia and near the Volga and Ural Rivers. Nearly half of the world's coal reserves are in Russia, with the largest coalfields in central and eastern Siberia. Although Russia has the world's largest deposits of mineral resources, many of these are difficult to extract because they are in remote areas with extreme weather conditions. Transportation to and from these remote areas is another big problem because there are often no roads or railroads near the resources.

▲ The Volga River is a key transportation route in the European part of Russia. Barges have always been used to transport heavy goods along this river and still play an important role in the Russian distribution system.

Russia's energy supply

Many rivers provide hydroelectric power stations, which produce nearly 20 percent of all Russia's electricity needs. Another 66 percent of Russian electricity comes from fossil fuel and the remaining 14 percent from nuclear power. There are plans to expand the nuclear industry so that it can power 25 percent of the home market by 2020.

▶ Constructed during the communist leader Stalin's rule, these huge buildings in Moscow are floodlit at night, making a magnificent sight, but using a lot of electricity.

Gas

Russia is fortunate enough to own about 40 percent of the world's reserves of natural gas. A large amount is sold to Western Europe. The Russian gas sector is dominated by a company called Gazprom, which is partly owned by the Russian government. Gazprom produces the vast majority of the country's natural gas and controls Russia's pipeline network. However, despite large oil deposits, domestic gas prices are rising.

▲ *The Gazprom headquarters in Moscow. Gazprom is Russia's main energy supplier and earns much foreign currency with its gas exports.*

IN THEIR OWN WORDS

My name is Artyom Vitalyevich. I live in Moscow and I work for Gazprom, one of the largest gas companies in the world. About 20 percent of the world's gas is provided by our company, which has the longest gas pipeline in the world and is one of the largest employers in the country. We supply gas to several countries abroad and are planning to extend our pipelines and increase our sales. Exports of gas are very important for the Russian economy. We are also investing a lot of money in ecological projects to make sure that no further damage is done to the environment.

Oil

Oil production is very important for Russia. It provides about 25 percent of the government's income and employs thousands of people. Transneft, the main Russian oil company, is not only a huge oil producer, but it is also the largest oil-transporting company in the world. The overall length of its pipeline is 29,800 miles (46,800 kilometers). This is longer than the length of the equator.

As the second-largest oil exporter in the world, after Saudi Arabia, Russia supplies about 13 percent of the world's oil. This is sold to many European countries. Many oil deposits have yet to be developed, so it is estimated that Russia's oil reserves will last for more than fifty years.

▲ The Trans-Siberian oil pipeline stretches thousands of miles through difficult and hostile landscape. There were many problems to overcome during its construction, and it requires constant maintenance.

◀ Russia is the world's second-largest oil producer and exports a large part of its crude oil production. Large refineries also supply the growing domestic market.

Forestry

About 25 percent of the world's forests are in Russia. However, Russia produces only 3 percent of the world's timber, because the forests are often in very inaccessible areas of the country. The country usually exports unfinished timber and then imports finished wood at a much higher price. At present, anybody can lease a forest for a period of five years. The government wants to grant licenses for up to 49 years.

IN THEIR OWN WORDS

My name is Katya Bochkova. I am 22. As a student, I took part in folklore expeditions. We traveled to the northern city of Archangelsko. I was amazed by the vastness of the forest there. When you fly over the taiga it seems it has no end—just a huge green expanse of forest. You can mainly see birch trees outside Moscow, but the taiga forest is very different—it is so thick and unspoiled. There are so many animals, including bears, foxes, and deer. I didn't see any bears, but I saw foxes and deer. I was also amazed to meet many professional hunters. They hunted animals and sold their furs. I had not imagined that people earned their livings this way.

Longer licenses will encourage investment and the building of factories so that timber can be processed and finished in Russia rather than abroad.

However, deforestation is a big issue for Russia. Thousands of acres of forests disappear each year. Some Russian experts believe that the forests will regrow naturally. However, ecologists believe that the rapid cutting of forests will contribute to climate change.

Renewable energy

Since the country has such abundant fossil fuels, so far little attention has been paid to alternative energy sources such as wind and solar power. Currently, there are few plans for developing sources of renewable energy.

▼ *The forests of central Russia are different from the taiga. The birch tree is a national Russian symbol.*

5 The Changing Environment

During Communism, every effort was made to improve industry and to produce enough food for the Soviet Union's people. Large amounts of money were spent on developing and producing weapons. Meanwhile, very little attention was paid to the environment. Industrial waste, fertilizers, pesticides, and untreated sewage flowed into rivers and lakes. Industry pumped carbon dioxide and other harmful substances into the atmosphere. Many years of neglect turned Russia into one of the most polluted countries in the world, and the pollution affected the environment and the health of people, animals, and plants. However, the government now has plans to develop an environmental policy.

▼ *Russia has more than 600 thermal power stations that use mainly gas. They join the rest of industry as polluters of the environment. However, cars remain the main cause of urban pollution.*

Air pollution
The Soviet Union was once the world's main air polluter. Air pollution is believed to be the main cause of global warming. Because of the reduction in industrial output since the collapse of the Soviet Union, the situation in Russia is now improving.

IN THEIR OWN WORDS

My name is Pavel and I am a biologist. As a young person, I am concerned about the cleanliness of the air that we breathe and the water we drink. In St. Petersburg, the air is very polluted. I have heard that Greenpeace has been campaigning in Russia since 1992, for example, against the cutting of forests in Karelia. It is very hard to fight against the big companies and the government, but I am glad that someone cares enough to try to do so. It was partly because of Greenpeace that places like Lake Baikal were made World Heritage Sites—sites of world importance.

The effects of Russia's industry mean that in some cities air pollution is up to ten times higher than the permitted level. Although air pollution in Moscow is less than in some other Russian cities, it is still about four times higher than it should be. In Soviet times, the government tried to move industry out of Moscow, but there was not enough money to build new factories elsewhere. Recently, measures have been taken to cut down on pollution in Moscow. Several factories have been closed and a local oil refinery has been ordered to stop burning off unwanted gas.

◄ *Many factories closed down after the collapse of the Soviet Union. However, industrial pollution in big cities is still a problem, and now these cities also have unemployment problems.*

Car pollution

In the Soviet Union, it was very difficult to buy a car because there was a long waiting list and prices were kept artificially high by the state. Today there are no waiting lists, private companies sell cars, and many people can afford to buy them. In addition to nearly two million cars in Moscow, about 200,000 people drive vehicles into the city every day. The downside is that private vehicles are currently the main air polluters in Russia. Car exhaust gases are responsible for 87 percent of all air pollution.

▲ *There are many old vehicles on Russian roads that pollute the air. Public transportation buses are much friendlier to the environment.*

In 1997, along with most of the world's countries, Russia signed the United Nation's Kyoto agreement. The aim of the agreement is to reduce greenhouse gases around the world by giving each country a pollution-reduction target.

Water pollution

Industrial pollution affects not only the air, but also the quality of drinking water. Rivers and seas are polluted when

◀ *This river is polluted from many years of environmental neglect during the Soviet period.*

◄ *Much of the Russian coastline has been polluted with industrial waste. Little money is spent on environmental care or protection.*

industrial waste is discharged directly into waterways. The Soviet authorities made little effort to regulate factories. In Russia, too, there are many examples of serious damage still being done to water quality. Even Lake Baikal has been badly affected. A further threat to water quality comes from old nuclear submarines that have been dumped on the northern coasts of Russia, and may be leaking nuclear waste into the seas.

IN THEIR OWN WORDS

My name is Lubov Semyonovna and I live in St. Petersburg. I am an administrator in the local government offices. Car pollution seems to be a big problem in our city. In the early 1990s, when many factories closed, the air was very clean. Even today, there are not many big factories that pollute the air. The main culprits are the cars on the road. Everybody complains about how hard life is, but the number of private cars has increased considerably in the last ten years. The roads are very congested. It seems to me that car pollution is getting worse every day.

Nuclear pollution

From the 1940s onward, the nuclear weapons and power industries were priorities for the Soviet government. Now there are huge stockpiles of nuclear waste in Russia—possibly as much as 220 million tons. When a nuclear reactor exploded at the Chernobyl nuclear energy plant in 1986 (in what is now the country of Ukraine), it polluted a large area of Europe—as far west as Wales. There have been other serious incidents at nuclear plants, for example, at Chelyabinsk in 1957, when the cooling system of a radioactive waste containment unit exploded.

Russia spent years building a huge underground nuclear reprocessing plant at Krasnoyarsk in Siberia. The government hopes to clear the backlog of nuclear waste and reprocess waste from other countries, for government income. The Duma—the Russian parliament—has ruled that any income from Krasnoyarsk will be used for projects to improve the environment.

▲ *In 1954 the Obninsk nuclear power plant was the first in the world to produce electricity. Today there are more than 50 nuclear power plants working in Russia.*

Ecology

Before 1991 environmental activists operated illegally because the government did not allow them freedom of speech. But today, more and more Russians are becoming aware of ecology—the study of living things and their environments. Since 1991, several ecological pressure groups have been founded. Because of their efforts, some positive changes have taken place in recent years.

Recycling and waste

Western-style packaging is becoming more popular, but it produces a lot more waste. At the moment, Russian society does not recycle much waste, which has become a problem. Environmental groups are trying to get people to recycle more materials, more often.

▲ *Russian winters are very cold. Even Lake Baikal, the deepest freshwater lake in the world, freezes over. A unique variety of plant and animal life is found in the lake's clear waters.*

IN THEIR OWN WORDS

My name is Larissa, and I am a 32-year-old psychologist. I am interested in ecology because it affects our health and our lives. I live in Voronezh. We have a big nuclear power station just outside our city. They were going to build another one, but the Chernobyl disaster made people more aware of the problems of nuclear power. Local people protested against the new station and the plans were scrapped. I think it was the right decision. I'm not sure what the alternative should be. Maybe we should use more hydroelectric power or more solar or wind power, but I am definitely against more nuclear power stations being built.

The Changing Population

Russia is the world's largest country, and population density in some regions is the lowest in the world. It is particularly low in the northern parts of Russia. The majority of Russians live in the European part of the country, west of the Ural Mountains. The Moscow region is especially crowded. This low population rate is a major concern for the Russian government, which believes having more people will help the country grow and prosper.

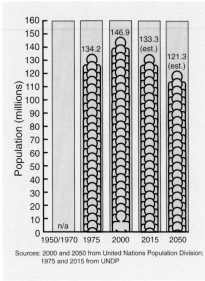

Sources: 2000 and 2050 from United Nations Population Division; 1975 and 2015 from UNDP

▲ *The Russian government is concerned about predictions that the country's population will decline sharply.*

◀ *New markets and shopping centers are opening up all over Russia. Although the overall population of Russia is shrinking, the number of people living in towns and cities is growing. Population density in Moscow is particularly high.*

Population Decline

The birth rate has been slowly decreasing for several decades, and in 1992, for the first time, more Russians died than were born. In 2001, the population fell by more than 500,000 people. There are several reasons for the decreasing population. The Russian birth rate is very low. In 2001 most families had only one child. The greater opportunities now available to Russians allows some families to choose to

◄ *This young Russian family is unusual, since many couples in Russia are waiting until later in life to have children.*

Another reason for the decrease is the high death rate among infants, due to poor health care in maternity hospitals. Increasing numbers of young people are dying because of drug and alcohol abuse. Stress-related diseases are on the rise as the population copes with unemployment and the loss of the social support that was available under Communism. Life expectancy has dropped since 1991. On average, male life expectancy is 59 years old (six years less than in 1991), while women's life expectancy is 72 years (down from 74 years old).

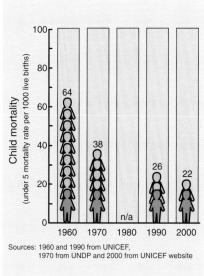

Sources: 1960 and 1990 from UNICEF,
1970 from UNDP and 2000 from UNICEF website

▲ *The mortality rate among children younger than 5 is dropping, but it is still very high.*

IN THEIR OWN WORDS

My name is Aza Hazbulatova. I am 29 and am from Ingushetia, in the south of Russia, next to Chechnya. I came to Moscow five years ago to live with my brother's family. Moscow is fantastic and I would like to stay here. There are many job opportunities here and lots of new businesses. I work in a travel agency and tourism is flourishing. I would eventually like to have two children, which is more than most families have these days, but I will wait until I am married before starting a family.

Immigration, emigration, and language

If Russian people were not returning to Russia from former Soviet republics, the population decline would be even more serious. During Soviet times, Russian was the official language—all Soviet citizens studied it and spoke it. However, Russians who had moved to the smaller republics did not usually speak the language of the republic they were living in.

In 1991, after the Soviet Union broke up and its republics became independent, each country revived its own national language. Many Russians suddenly became foreigners in these new countries. Language difficulties meant that some people could not find work, and so they returned to Russia. The influx of people into Russia has put pressure on housing and social services in some parts of the country, especially in the capital, Moscow.

A diverse population

On December 1, 2001, there were 145 million people in Russia. Among them are 120 million Russians, 5.5 million Tatars, 4.4 million Ukrainians, 1.8 million Chuvashi, and more than 80 other ethnic groups that inhabit Russia's huge territory. The Communist government of the Soviet Union did not approve of religion.

▼ *Takhir, from Tajikistan, sells dried fruit, fish, and nuts at the market in Moscow.*

IN THEIR OWN WORDS

My name is Roman Tutsuda, and I am an archpriest in the Orthodox Church. Since 1988, when religion was permitted, the authorities have stopped interfering in Church affairs. Today, many young people go to church and several Orthodox schools have been founded. Priests are also allowed to visit schools, hospitals, and military units to talk with people there. The Church is becoming more active in the lives of Russians. Our main concern is the spiritual, the inner world, of a person. But we have only had a few years of freedom to make up for more than seventy years of oppression, and there is still much to do.

But Orthodox Christianity, the main religion in Russia, survived Communism and is now enjoying a period of growth. In addition different faiths, such as Islam, are growing among the diverse population.

◀ *The Cathedral of Christ the Savior was rebuilt in the late 1990s, after being demolished by Communists in the 1930s. Many new places of worship have been opened by the Russian Orthodox Church since the collapse of the Soviet Union.*

7 Changes at Home

The collapse of the Soviet Union and its systems has brought more opportunities and choices to Russian people, but has also changed the balance in some households.

Young people

Today, young Russians are not in a hurry to start families. First, they want to see the world or develop their careers. They have opportunities that their parents could only dream of. Living standards are improving for some. Foreign travel is easier, shops offer more choices, and career opportunities are much more exciting.

Most of the Soviet youth organizations that used to occupy young people in their spare time and during vacations are gone. Instead, there are discos and clubs. A lot of young people now have part-time jobs to earn enough money to pay for their lifestyles.

▼ *Young people in post-Soviet Russia now enjoy the same pastimes, music, and fashions as their counterparts in the West.*

IN THEIR OWN WORDS

My name is Natasha, and I am 24. I was born in the Perm region near the Ural Mountains, but I came to Moscow to study in the Chemical Institute. I have a degree in chemistry, but a chemical engineer's salary is very small; it is impossible to survive on it. I earn more by selling souvenirs. I think it was easier for our parents because their homes were given to them by the state. Today, you have to work all your life to earn enough money for even a very small apartment. In the future, I would like to train and work as a makeup artist and have a family.

◀ *Many stores stock luxury items for wealthy "New Russians" to buy.*

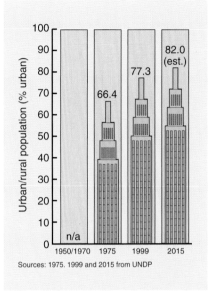

Sources: 1975. 1999 and 2015 from UNDP

The "New Russians"

In the past, the state owned everything, but now Russians are allowed to own property. Many people are buying houses and condos. During the first years after Communism, some people became rich very quickly and are known as the "New Russians." Most people would agree that their lives are better than in Soviet times, but they feel there is great pressure on them to earn enough to support their lifestyles.

▲ *This graph shows that Russia is rapidly becoming a much more urban society.*

▼ *A lot of expensive* dachas, *or summer country houses, have been built in recent years. A new generation of successful Russian entrepreneurs and business people can afford houses like this one.*

Education

In the Soviet Union, education was free, but it was controlled by the state. All schools had the same curriculums and textbooks, and all the same subjects were required. Nearly 70 percent of Soviet children went to nursery schools or kindergartens that were partly paid for by the state. After 1991, the state nursery schools quickly disappeared. Parents had to make other arrangements, such as paying for private day care or asking family members for help. Today the majority of schools and educational establishments need new equipment and facilities. More than half of all parents have to contribute financially to their childrens' education.

Changes also have been made to the classes. Textbooks on history, politics, religion, and the economy—written from the Soviet point of view—have been updated. Older students can now choose which subjects to study, but there is often a shortage of teachers, especially for new subjects such as information technology.

▲ Many Russian grandparents look after their grandchildren. The Soviet Union provided partially subsidized nursery schools for all children, but these have largely disappeared from modern Russia.

◄ Teaching is still a largely female profession.

IN THEIR OWN WORDS

My name is Nadezhda Anatolyevna, and I live in Tver. This is a large town on the main road from Moscow to St. Petersburg. I am a grandmother. I have a son, a daughter, and three grandchildren. Today, I'm looking after Mishka, my 19-month-old grandchild. I used to work in a bakery, but I retired two years ago. It's just as well I'm not working. There are no state nursery schools anymore and private child care is very expensive. Grandparents have to help their children any way they can, so I take care of my grandchildren while my children go to work.

Private schools now exist, but the vast majority of students still go to state-run schools. A small percentage of children, especially those of well-off parents, are sent to study in boarding schools abroad.

Higher education

Over half of all college students pay for their educations. The most popular subjects are economics and accounting. Universities now set their own entrance exams. However, there are plans to introduce a single examination so that all students can apply to the universities of their choice. Many hope this will reduce cheating and bribery in university entry procedures.

▶ *Moscow State University is one of the oldest universities in Russia. It was founded in 1755.*

The armed forces

In Russia, national service in the armed forces is compulsory for 18-year-old men. However, serving in the armed forces is unpopular because of the difficult living conditions and the controvesial Chechen conflict in the south of Russia. Many try to get out of service with fake medical certificates. The government is now trying to introduce an alternative of community service for those people whose beliefs do not allow them to serve in the armed forces.

Since Soviet times, Russia has halved its armed forces. The country still has about a million conscripts and professional officers, but that is still too many soldiers to clothe and feed. Proposals are being discussed to reduce the army even more by doing away with forced national service. Russia is also seeking closer links with NATO, so that Russia can become more involved with international peacekeeping initiatives.

▲ *It is prestigious to serve as a guard at the Moscow Kremlin. This is the heart of Russian government and a long way from the troubles in Chechnya in the south.*

IN THEIR OWN WORDS

Our names are Evgeny and Oleg. We're cadets in the Engineering Naval College—we're going to be naval officers and serve in the Russian Northern Fleet. In order to become a naval officer you need to study for five years. This is our first year. So far, we've had to pass exams in math, physics, Russian, and fitness. The Russian fleet is becoming stronger, and we are proud that in the future we are going to defend our country. In five to ten years, we're sure that everything will be better in Russia.

Health care

Since the early 1990s, a two-tier system of health care has developed in Russia. There are many well-staffed private hospitals with the latest technology; however, state hospitals are usually short of medicine and equipment, because the state cannot fund them properly.

A health care insurance system, paid for with contributions from people's salaries, was introduced in 1993, but the money collected is not enough to cover medical costs. Consultations with family doctors remain free, but people usually have to pay for any treatments.

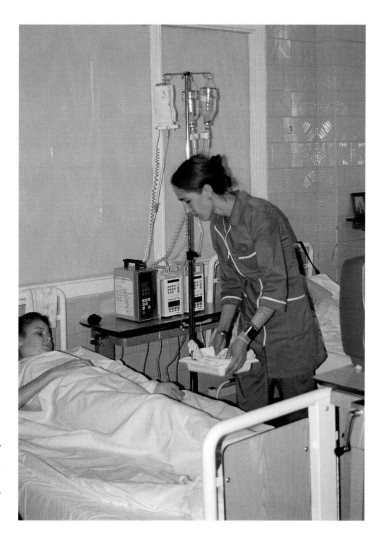

▶ *Some Russian hospitals are doing better than others. This hospital for sick children has good modern equipment and is one of the best in St. Petersburg.*

Food and shopping

When Russia was part of the Soviet Union, most people were not able to buy even oranges or bananas. Shops sold basic food and consumer goods, but choice was limited. People sometimes had to line up for several hours to buy essentials, such as potatoes, sugar, or bread. Since then, there have been great changes in shopping in Russia. In bigger towns, there are many more supermarkets and shopping centers, and a range of items for sale that were never available in Soviet times, especially luxury items.

At the beginning of the 1990s, the government used oil revenue to buy large amounts of foreign goods and food. Anything foreign was very popular. Today things have changed. Shopping for food and other goods is much easier—there are no lines and shops are well stocked. People have more confidence in Russian-made food and goods because the quality has improved. However, many people still cannot afford adequate amounts of food. A large percentage of households rely on small urban gardens to provide them with fresh fruits and vegetables.

▲ *This shopping mall in Moscow has many designer shops.*

▲ *As these pictures show, eating out is very popular in Russia today and there are many new cafés, fast-food stands, and restaurants.* ▶

Window-shopping is a new hobby in Russia. Recently, expensive designer shops, both foreign and Russian, have opened, but their prices are often too expensive for most people. There are also now restaurants and eating places to suit any taste and budget. A restaurant meal was always a popular way for Russians to celebrate, and this remains the case today.

IN THEIR OWN WORDS

We are road sweepers and it is our lunch break now. Some of us have been doing this job for 20 years. We don't like the job but it pays a salary, and we can retire at the age of 55. We work from 8 A.M. untill 4 P.M. Work is harder now—there is more litter and dirt on the roads. Still, shopping is much easier today than it was in the past. We used to spend most of our time in lines trying to buy food or shoes or clothes. Today it is very easy. You can buy everything. There are many restaurants, cafés, and other places to eat, too, but we can only afford to eat out on special occasions.

Sports

Sports were very important in Soviet times, but there are now fewer opportunities to play team sports. State funding of youth organizations has been reduced or has disappeared altogether. Even large towns have few facilities. At the same time, many private—and expensive—health clubs have opened. They are often in remote areas that are accessible only by car. Although the government is trying to encourage all Russians to take up sports again, it remains to be seen whether they will be successful.

▲ *Students enjoy sports after lectures at Moscow State University. The Russian government is encouraging young people to play more sports.*

◄ *Soccer is a very popular spectator sport in Russia, but it is mainly played during summer months. Ice hockey is more popular in winter.*

Leisure

In the Soviet Union, Western popular music was not allowed because the government was afraid that Western ideas would corrupt young citizens' minds. Now, if they want to, young people are free to have the same interests, listen to the same music, and follow the same fashions as young people living in the West. Many Russian music groups are also very successful, and some have enjoyed international success. There are plenty of venues that play music, and some are open all day and all night.

The Internet keeps young people up to date with the latest news and developments around the globe. The number of homes with Internet access is increasing. Many talented Russian computer programmers are helping the country's computer industry to develop rapidly and catch up with the West.

▶ *Inline skating is not as popular in Russia as it is in the U.S., but it is growing in popularity. Unfortunately, safety helmets and protective gear are still rare.*

IN THEIR OWN WORDS

My name is Tanya. I am a student. I think young people in Russia have the same interests as young people abroad. I like to go see modern music. We have some really good venues with all the latest Russian and Western music. I keep up with the latest music and fashion news on the Internet. My boyfriend is a Web designer and programmer. He has a lot of work and is well paid for it. He recently joined a health club but doesn't go there often because it is a long drive out of town. I know I don't exercise enough. I played sports at school but there is nowhere for me to play sports near where I live.

8

Changes at Work

For more than 70 years, life was centrally planned and controlled in the Soviet Union. A government committee decided everything that the country produced—from nails to vegetables. The price of each product was also set by a committee. The result was that a spoon, for example, cost exactly the same no matter where it was bought throughout the fifteen Soviet republics.

Officially, there was no inflation, unemployment, or workers' strikes. In reality, much of Soviet industry was inefficient and made poor-quality products. Huge plants and factories that produced goods for the whole Soviet Union ensured that all regions of the Soviet Union depended on one another. When the Soviet Union collapsed, the links between the regions was broken and the economy also collapsed.

▲ *Since the collapse of the Soviet Union, many private banks have opened up in Russia.*

Difficult changes

The change from a centrally controlled and planned economy to a market economy in which goods are sold between different regions and prices go up and down according to demand, was neither easy nor quick. There was often no money to pay people's salaries for several months, and some workers were paid with the goods they produced. Many plants and factories had to close, and much of the manufacturing industry later failed because it was making outdated and poor-quality goods that could not compete with cheap, better-quality imports.

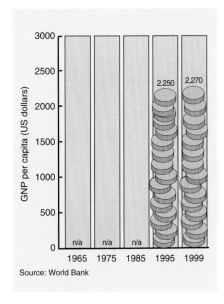

Source: World Bank

▲ *This graph shows that there was only a small rise in the income per person in Russia from 1995 to 1999.*

Freedom of the press

The collapse of the Soviet Union brought big changes in the Russian media. Many new radio and TV stations and newspapers were started. A new generation of journalists replaced those of the Soviet era. The new journalists had more freedom to express their opinions.

► *Although it is very good, the public transportation system cannot cope with everyone who needs to travel. Private car owners are often willing to be flagged down and give people rides.*

IN THEIR OWN WORDS

My name is Andrey, and I am 29. I studied journalism at Moscow State University. I know that for journalists in Soviet times there were many restrictions and no freedom of speech. However, when I started work, it was a time of opportunities in the Russian media, because many older journalists preferred to leave the profession rather than adapt. Many new TV channels and newspapers appeared but not all of them survived. Life keeps changing all the time. I don't like all the changes, but I look forward to the future with optimism because I am optimistic by nature.

The road to recovery

In 1991 the government allowed prices for all goods to be set by the people who sell them. Prices soared, but salaries did not, so Russia saw its first strikes in more than 70 years.

The period between 1989 and 1998 was a very difficult one because industrial production and trade in Russia fell by 44 percent. However, the economy is slowly recovering. The new market economy aims to produce what people want at prices they can afford. More factories are producing goods needed in everyday life, such as food, clothes, and items for the home. Information technology and the service and construction industries are booming, and unemployment has fallen to 8 percent of the workforce.

▲ *The harsh Russian climate takes its toll on Russian roads. The recovering economy helps repairs to be made more regularly than they were in the 1990s.*

Private business

In 1991 people were first allowed to start their own companies. One year later, there were nearly 200,000 private businesses. Now about 35 percent of the workforce is employed by small businesses rather than the state. Private companies cover all spheres of life: building, industry,

◄ *New buildings are going up all over Russia. It is now possible to buy and sell an apartment or house, which was not the case in the Soviet Union.*

agriculture, health care, and retailing. Consumers now have a choice of whom to buy from, and companies rely on customer satisfaction for their future business. As a result, customer service is better and the quality of goods has improved. Whether they are buying meat at the market or hiring a plumber, Russian consumers can now expect good value for their money.

▶ *The telecommunications revolution has reached Russia, too, and many people regularly use cellular phones. New public telephones also are being installed, but using up-to-date phone cards rather than coins.*

IN THEIR OWN WORDS

My name is Sasha. This is my wife, Sveta, and our two-year-old son, Misha. I used to work as a taxi driver and my wife worked as a clerk in a bank. Today, we have our own business. We started selling beverages wholesale more than five years ago and our company is now doing very well. We have a couple of large trucks and employ about ten people. Of course, there is a lot of stress, especially with keeping records of sales and orders, but the more you work the more money you earn. I also like being my own boss. Life is not bad at the moment, but we would prefer to have a clearer tax policy and better retirement funds.

Agriculture

After the collapse of the Soviet Union, agriculture was affected badly. The farms could not cope with the new demands of the market. There were not enough farmworkers, because many young people left to find jobs in cities. In 1990, a law was passed that allowed people to buy land. Six years later, there were nearly 300,000 small farms in Russia. And, unlike the old state-owned farms, the farms could sell their product for profit and support themselves.

▼ *Small private farms usually do not have up-to-date machinery. Profits from production should make it possible now for private farmers to start investing in modern equipment.*

Farming in Russia is developing and improving slowly. More efficient use is being made of the land, and the quality of produce is rising. A lack of resources means that Russian farmers tend not to use many chemical fertilizers and pesticides, so vegetables and meat are relatively organic. Russia still has to import some food, but it is self-sufficient in all the basics.

IN THEIR OWN WORDS

My name is Michael. I am 63 years old. Two years ago I retired from my job in the factory where I worked for 40 years. My pension is not very big, and prices have gone up a lot. I work now for this small farm. The work is not easy; all the equipment is old and they don't always pay us on time. Only retirees work here. The younger generation doesn't want to work on the land anymore. The things we produce are good quality and easy enough to sell, so I hope the farm will continue to do well. They are changing the way we pay taxes, and I do not suppose that will leave us with much money in our pockets.

Paying for Russia's future

A new system of taxation has been a priority for the government. If the Russian government does not collect enough taxes to pay for the running of the country, the country will experience serious difficulties. In 2002, a new tax system was introduced. A big publicity campaign was launched to encourage workers to pay taxes and ensure that Russia's future is well funded.

▼ *These are typical residential buildings. The majority of people in Russia live in apartments.*

Women

Women make up more than half of the Russian population and, since the collapse of the Soviet Union, life has become more difficult for them in some ways. They are often the first to be unemployed, because companies are anxious to avoid paying for maternity leave, which is quite generous in Russia. On the other hand, the changes that have taken place in Russia have also given women opportunities to develop their careers, improve their standards of living, and become more independent. Many women have opened new businesses and become managers and directors of companies. However, women have lost some ground as politicians. Under the

▲ *Some mothers stay at home to look after their children because free state day care is no longer available.*

▲ *Women have new opportunities to start their own businesses or develop their careers. It is increasingly common to see a woman in charge of a company.*

Communist system they were guaranteed almost 33 percent of political positions, but now they occupy about 16 percent of the seats in the Duma, Russia's parliament.

Tourism

In Soviet times, the authorities did not want their citizens to have the freedom to travel abroad. Only a very privileged few, usually Communist party members, were allowed out

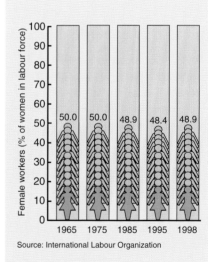

▲ *The number of women who work as a percentage of the entire working population has not changed much since Soviet times*

IN THEIR OWN WORDS

My name is Youlya, and I am 32. I work for a travel agency. My job is challenging and very interesting. I organize many trips abroad and some trips around Russia. Foreign tourists are more educated today. They don't think any more that there are bears on the street. The number of foreign tourists coming to this country and Russian tourists going abroad is increasing. What we need to do now is to develop better communications with other parts of Russia and build more good hotels in places of interest.

of the country. This changed when Russia became independent. Since then, over 15,000 travel agencies have opened. The improving economy also means that many Russians now have more money to spend on vacations. With their newly opened borders, Russian tourists have traveled all over the world.

The number of foreign tourists visiting Russia fell after the collapse of the Soviet Union. Visitors worried that Russia was dangerous, but they are now gradually returning. Tourists can now enjoy a broad choice of vacations, from salmon fishing in Siberia to museums in St. Petersburg.

▶ *Tourists on a boat trip in St. Petersburg*

9

The Way Ahead

Much has changed in Russia and much more can still change in the future. Russia still has a long way to go to reach prosperity. Pollution of the environment could lead to climate change, and car use and industry are causing increasing damage to air and water quality. Natural resources are being exploited widely and rapidly, and the population is shrinking.

However, there have also been many positive changes since the collapse of the Soviet Union. There are new freedoms for people and for private companies, and Russian consumers now get much more for their money. Apart from the Chechen conflict, Russia has largely avoided the political and civil conflicts that some other Eastern European countries have suffered. The government has survived a number of economic crises and has kept the economy going. Finances have also improved, not only through economic growth but also because more people are paying taxes.

During their history Russians have lived through many hardships. However, Russians remain energetic and resilient, positive and inventive, and are determined to make their country a good place to live.

▲ A future generation of music lovers plays on a monument to the famous Russian composer Sergey Rachmaninoff (1873–1943).

◄ The Internet is widely available and very popular with young Russians. About 10 percent of Russians are regular Internet users, and the number is steadily rising.

IN THEIR OWN WORDS

My name is Alexander Tsvetayev. I am 17 years old and a pupil at a state high school. My favorite subjects are English language and math. I spend most of my free time on my computer. After I leave school, I want to go on to study information technology and become a computer programmer. I think life is improving in Russia—we just need more time and good government. I trust our government and think that our president is exactly what our country needs. We have problems, but I am sure that we can solve them in the near future.

With its vast resources and highly educated population, Russia can look to the future with considerable hope. A lot remains to be done, but this is a country that has come a long way since it left the Soviet Union. It has every chance of remaining an important country in the 21st century.

▼ *These girls finished school with a gold medal for top grades in their class. They are being honored with a party organized by the mayor of Moscow.*

Glossary

Bolshevik member of a Communist revolutionary group, led by Vladimir Lenin. The Bolsheviks seized power during the 1917 Russian Revolution.

Chechen conflict ongoing war in southwestern Russia. The area of Chechnya declared its independence in 1991.

Communism theory and system of social and political organization in which property is owned by the entire community as a whole rather than by individuals

coniferous describes a forest of primarily evergeen trees and bushes

conscript someone who has been required by the state to serve in the armed forces, rather than a volunteer or professional soldier

deforestation cutting down trees for the timber industry or for fuel, reducing forest cover

ecology study of the relationship of plants and animals to their physical and biological environment

economy community's system of using its resources to produce wealth

emigration people leaving their own country to live elsewhere

hydroelectric power electricity generated from turbines that are turned by the force of falling water

glasnost policy of more openness and less secrecy introduced by Mikhail Gorbachev in the Soviet Union in the mid-1980s

greenhouse gases gases in the atmosphere believed to trap heat from the Earth's surface and so contribute to global warming

immigration people coming to live in a country that is not their native land

inflation decline in the value of money in relation to the goods it can buy

Kyoto Protocol agreement signed by many countries in 1997 in Kyoto, Japan, that requires industrialized countries to reduce their emissions of greenhouse gases by 2012

market economy economic system in which individuals, rather than the state, make decisions about what to produce and how to sell it, responding to what consumers want to buy

national service period of time during which people are required by the state to serve in the armed forces or some other service that benefits the country

NATO (North Atlantic Treaty Organization) international organization established in 1949 to promote mutual defense and collective security that has been the primary Western military alliance since World War II

natural resources mineral and other deposits formed by natural processes that can be used for energy and other purposes

perestroika policy of government restructuring introduced by Mikhail Gorbachev to try to reform the Soviet Union in the mid-1980s

permafrost permanently frozen soil

renewable energy energy such as wind or wave power that is derived from natural forces rather than fuels such as coal that can only be burned once

republic state in which power belongs to the people rather than to a royal family

Soviet Union state founded after the Russian Revolution, run by the Communist party and made up of 15 republics. It covered 17 percent of the world's land surface, with a population of about 240 million people.

steppe vast grassy plains

taiga coniferous forest region of northern Russia and Siberia

tsar Russian king, or head of the Russian royal family

World Heritage Site area (or building) that possesses significant value to the entire world. Sites are selected by a United Nations committee.

Further Information

Books

Allan, Tony. *The Russian Revolution.* Chicago: Heinemann, 2003.

Downing, David. *Vladmir Ilyich Lenin.* Chicago: Heinemann, 2002.

Gottfried, Ted. *The Road to Communism.* Brookfield, Conn.: 21st Century Books, 2002.

Ross, Stewart. *The Russian Revolution.* Chicago: Raintree, 2003.

Wilson, Neil. *Russia.* Chicago: Raintree, 2001.

Useful addresses

Embassy of the Russian Federation
2650 Wisconsin Ave. NW
Washington, D.C. 20007
(202) 298-5700
www.russianembassy.org

United States Embassy in Russia
Bolshy Deviatinsky Pereulok
8 Moscow 121099
Russian Federation
www.usembassy.ru

Index

Page numbers in **bold** refer to photographs, maps, or charts.